Which Vowel Sound?

Look at the pictures and decide which ones cor_____ ____d.
If a word contains a short vowel sound, colour ____

e

u

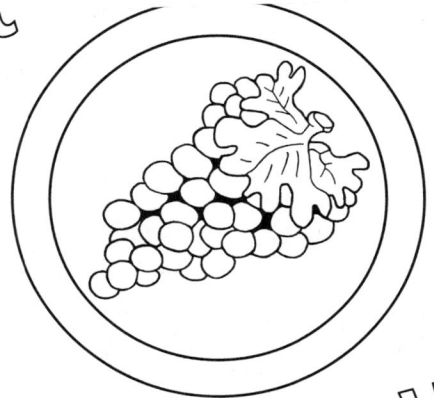

a
i
u

e

o
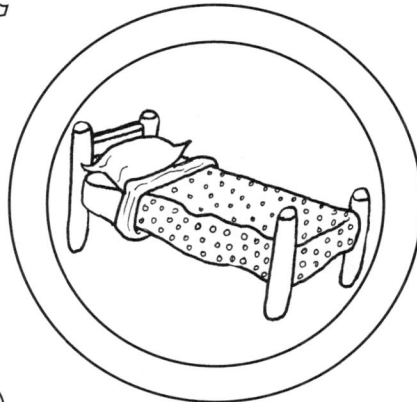

a

e

o

o

i
i

ay

ay ay ay
ay ay ay

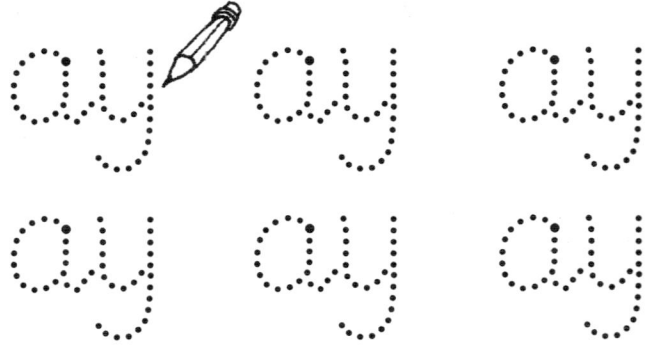

Add the missing ‹ay› to each word.
Then colour the crayons.

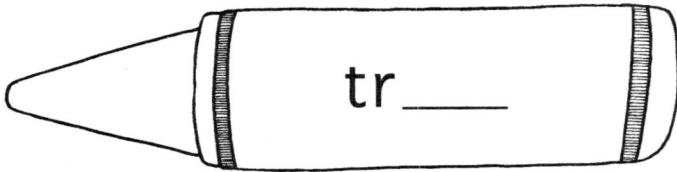

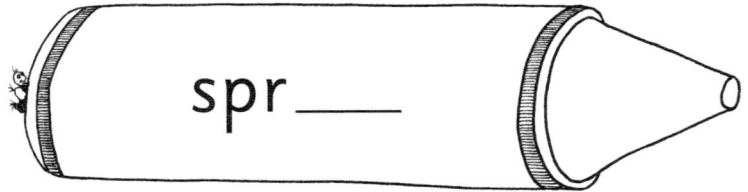

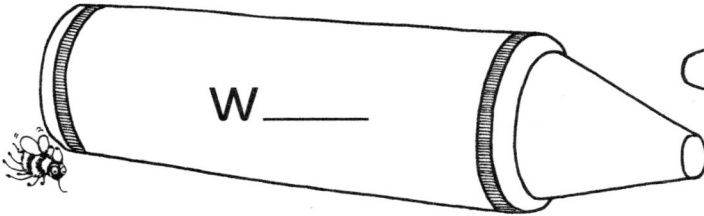

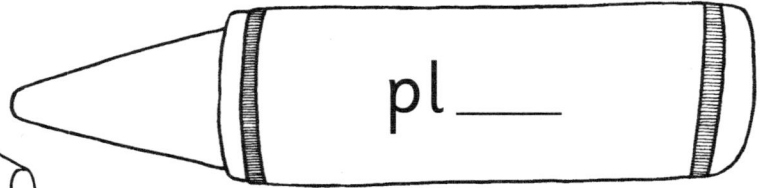

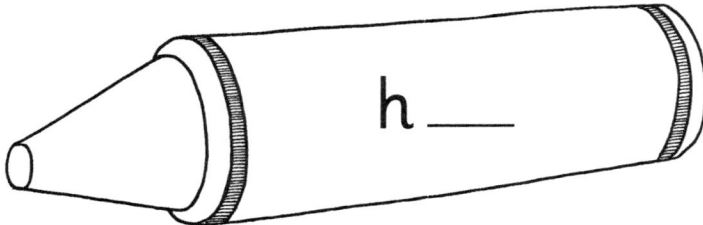

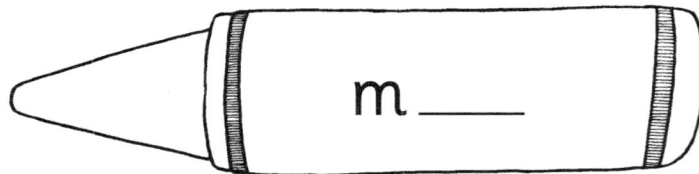

tr___

spr___

w___

pl___

h___

st___

m___

2

Days of the Week

Black

Write over the dotted words and then complete the sentences.

Monday   On Monday I _____
                _____

Tuesday   On Tuesday I _____
                _____

Wednesday   On Wednesday I _____
                _____

Thursday   On Thursday I _____
                _____

Friday   On Friday I _____
                _____

Saturday   On Saturday I _____
                _____

Sunday   On Sunday I _____
                _____

Alphabet Colours

Write the alphabet in lower case letters, using the four colour groups.

red

yellow

green

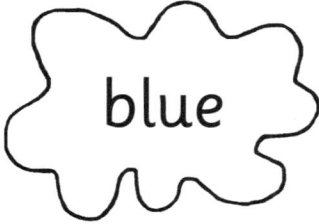
blue

a

Choose your favourite colour and write the alphabet again. This time, time yourself. How fast can you do it? Write your time in the watch.

Put these words into alphabetical order.

1.　　　　tractor　　car　　leaf

_____　　_____　　_____

2.　　　　pen　　quill　　crayon

_____　　_____　　_____

3.　　　Thursday　　Friday　　Saturday

_____　　_____　　_____

4.　　　　green　　blue　　yellow

_____　　_____　　_____

5.　　　tadpole　　painful　　useless

_____　　_____　　_____

ea

Action: Put your hands on your head, like a donkey pointing its ears up, and say *ee*.

ea   ea   ea

ea   ea   ea

Read the words and phrases and illustrate them in the teapots and steam.

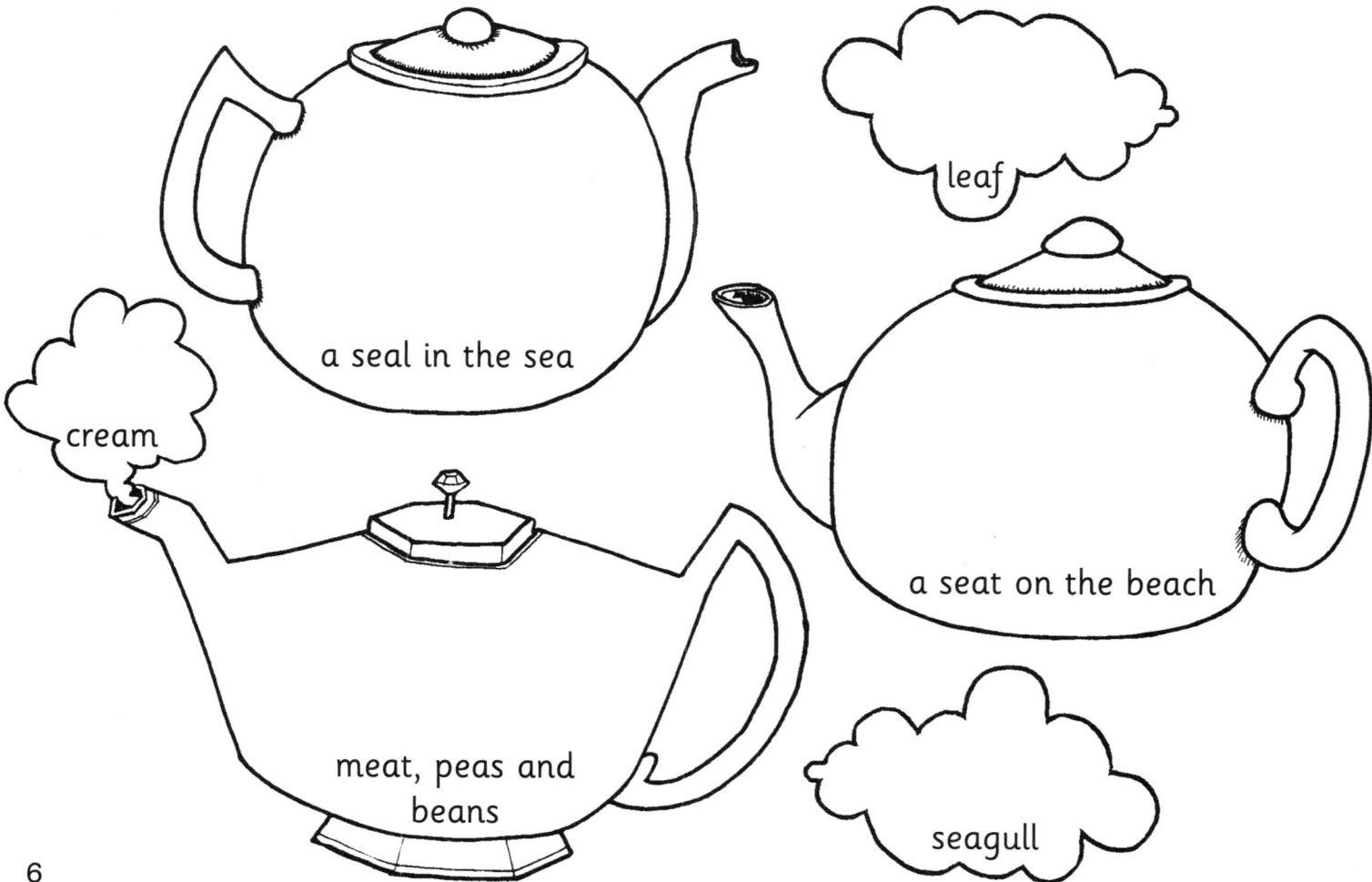

leaf

a seal in the sea

cream

a seat on the beach

meat, peas and beans

seagull

Past, Present and Future

Write the verbs in the past tense and in the future.

Verbs  Red

 past

 present

 future

past	present	future
I reached	I reach	I will reach
you _____	you stay	you ____ _____
he _____	he snaps	he ____ _____
she _____	she flops	she ____ _____
it _____	it fades	it ____ _____
I _____	I bake	I ____ _____
you _____	you like	you ____ _____
he _____	he claps	he ____ _____
she _____	she looks	she ____ _____
it _____	it rains	it ____ _____

7

Nouns

Look at the picture, find some common nouns and write them on the lines. **Nouns** can have the words 'a', 'an' or 'the' before them.

an _____   a _____   a _____

the _____   the _____   the _____

Parsing Nouns

Read the sentences and underline the **nouns** in black. Then draw a picture of each noun.

Black

1. The stripy <u>mug</u> is on the <u>rug</u>.

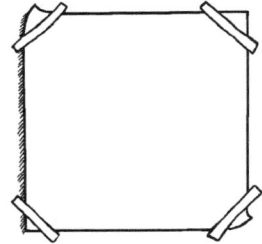

2. We collected the leaves.

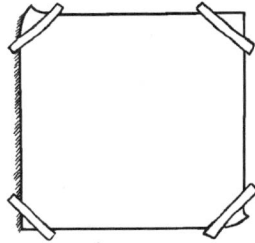

3. She has a big drink.

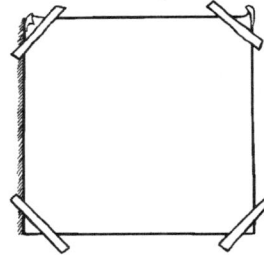

4. I have enjoyed a very good lunch.

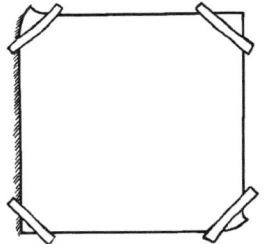

5. He ate too many chips.

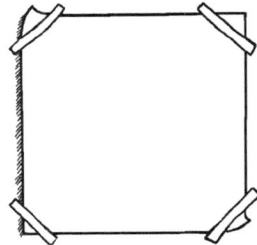

6. We went to the beach.

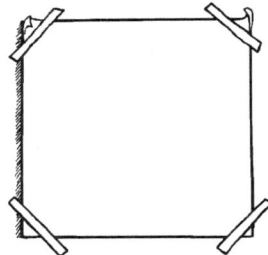

9

igh

Action: Stand to attention and salute, saying *ie, ie*.

igh   igh   igh

Remember, the sound /ie/ can also be spelt ‹ie›, as in *tie*, *pie*, *lie* and *die*, and ‹i_e›, as in *bike*, *like* and *kite*.

Read the words. Remember, there is a dot under each letter sound.

night   light   bright   high   fright

Write a sentence using as many ‹igh› words as you can.

_____

Draw a picture to illustrate your sentence in the box below.

Alphabetical Order

Write the words in alphabetical order.

1.   way   play   day   tray

_____ _____ _____ _____

2.   sea   leaf   tea   beach

_____ _____ _____ _____

3.   night   bright   thigh   sigh

_____ _____ _____ _____

4.   kite   like   bike   slide

_____ _____ _____ _____

Adjective Snakes

Read these adjectives:

blue	flowery
spotted	happy
bright	wet
old	long
fluffy	green

Adjectives are words that describe nouns.

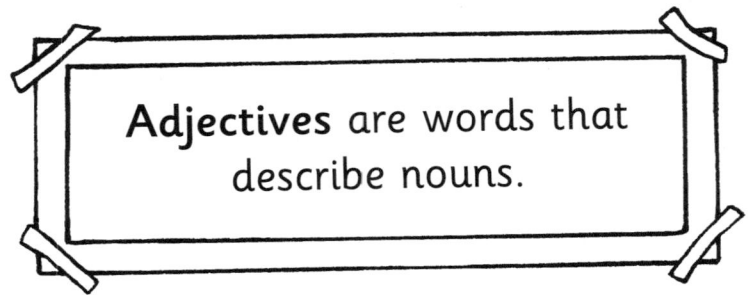

Choose your favourite **adjectives** and write one in each label. Then decorate the snakes to match the adjectives.

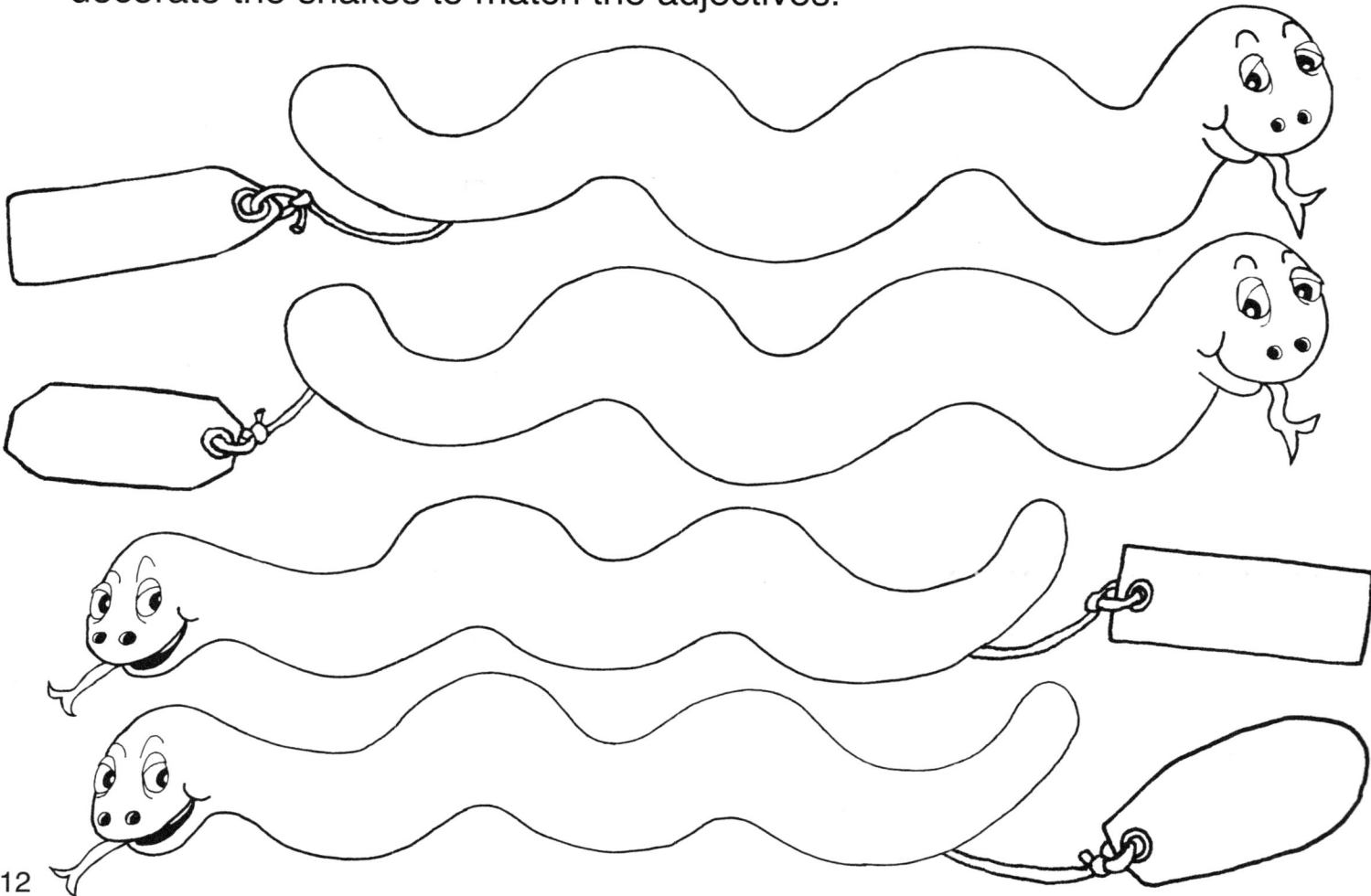

Initial and Final Consonant Blends

Match each consonant blend to the correct picture.

sk-

-lb

-nt

st-

sp-

-ld

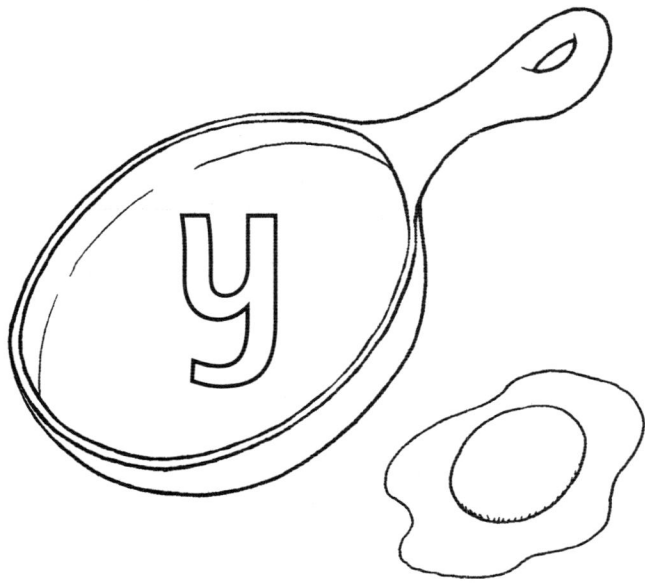

y

fry   try   sky

dry   my   fly

Complete the sentences using the ‹y› words above.

1. Planes _____ very high.

2. I can see the stars in the _____ .

3. They _____ the wet dog.

4. _____ scarf is blue and green.

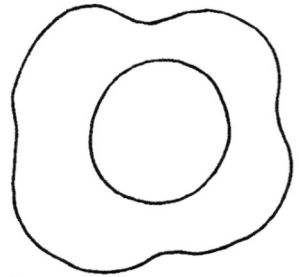

5. I _____ an egg for my lunch.

6. I _____ to play the flute.

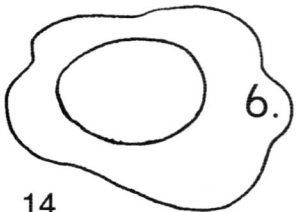

14

ie   i_e   igh   y

Look at the pictures and write the words.

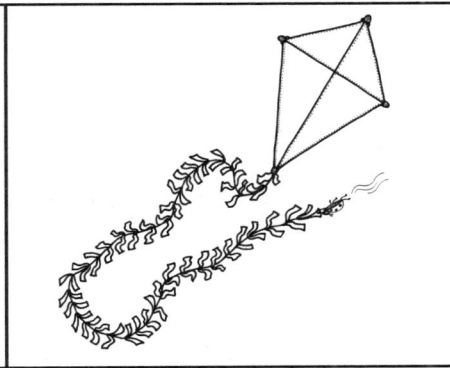

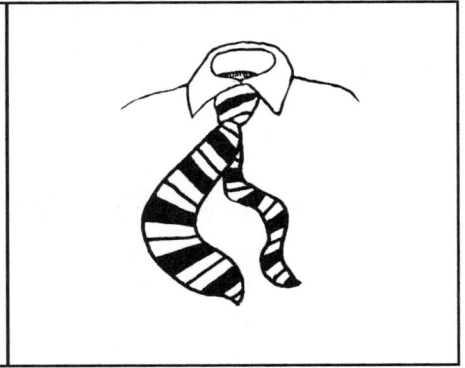

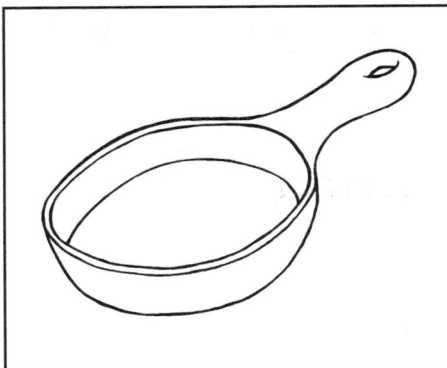

Write an **adjective** in each tower (choose from those below or think of your own). Decorate each tower to match the adjective.

yellow   new   black

dotty   spooky   pink

stripy   chilly   wet

dark   shiny   purple

white   red   hot

Action: Touch the side of your temple with your fist.

Parsing Adjectives and Nouns

Underline the **adjectives** in blue and the **nouns** in black.

Blue   Black

1. I have a <u>fluffy</u> <u>cat</u>.

2. We played with the red car.

3. They had a big cake.

4. It was a dark night.

5. He got a new bike.

6. She wins first prize.

7. I saw some little tadpoles.

8. We grew a white rose.

Action: Bring your hand over your mouth, as if something has gone wrong, and say *oh!*

ow   ow   ow

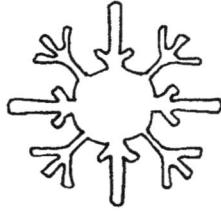
ow   ow   ow

Look at the pictures and write a word for each one.

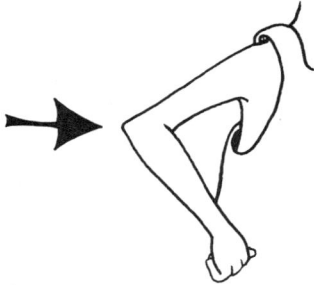

_____   _____   _____

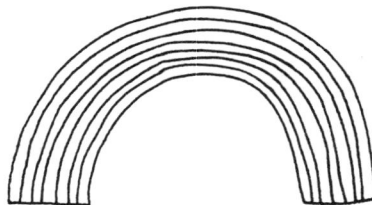

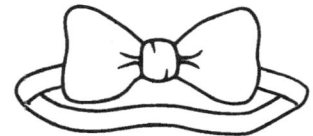

_____   _____   _____

Draw a snowman in the winter scene. Give him a name and write some sentences about him.

The snowman's name is _____

_____

_____

_____

_____

_____

ew

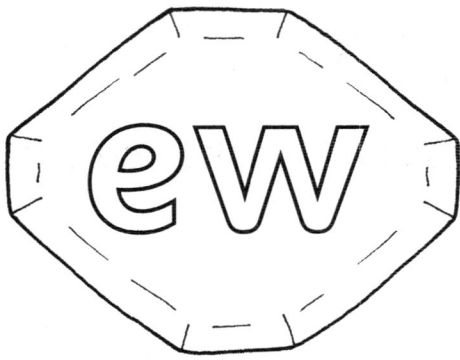

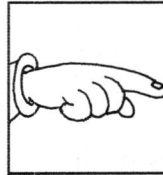

Action: Point to people around you and say *you, you, you.*

Action: Move your head forward like the cuckoo in a cuckoo clock, saying *oo.*

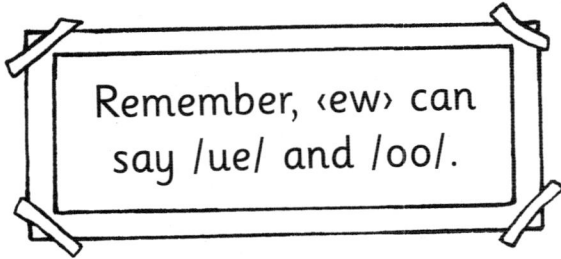

Remember, ‹ew› can say /ue/ and /oo/.

skew   skewer

few   fewer

Read the words and draw the pictures.

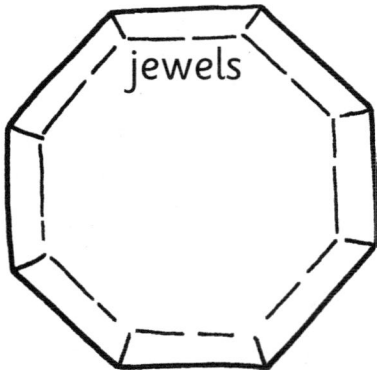

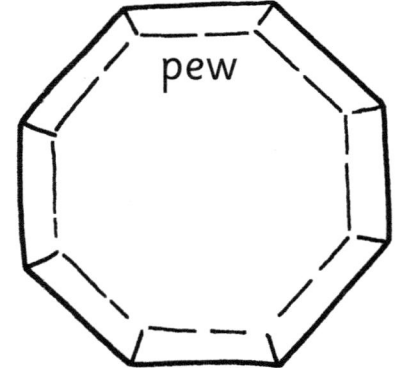

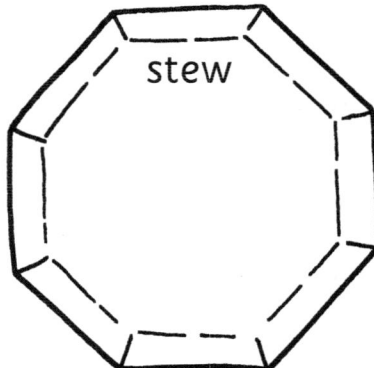

jewels

newt

pew

corkscrew

stew

newspaper

Colours of the Rainbow

Write over the dotted letters using the correct colours and then colour in the picture.

silver

black

white

red

orange

yellow

green

blue

purple

gold

Read the words, decide whether they are singular or plural, and draw a picture for each one.

cats	cobwebs	teacup
tadpoles	bride	dolls
windmill	broomstick	kites

Compound Birds

Complete the compound words by matching the birds' bodies to the correct tails.

cow

paper

speed

boy

news

fish

gold

boat

Tricky Question Words

wh   wh   wh   wh   wh

Write a sentence using each of the tricky question words and decorate the page with colourful question marks.

What _____

Why _____

When _____

Where _____

Who _____

Which _____

Write over the dotted letters to complete the tricky words.

any
other

many
were

more
because

before
want